Wedding Planner

3rd Edition

43 Elegant Wedding Crafts You Can Use for Center Pieces, Flowers, Decorations, And Much More!

by Kitty Moore

Table of Contents

Introduction

The importance of the wedding day in a person's life cannot be stressed enough. It is the one-day when you want every single small or big thing to go exactly as planned.

People say that the wedding day is the most beautiful day in your life. While that holds true for most people, it goes without saying that wedding days are the most stressful for almost every single individual. Not only do you have to digest the amazing fact that you are going to get married, but you also have to make preparations that do not fall short of your or anybody else's expectations.

You may ease the burden on your shoulders slightly by hiring a world-class wedding planner, but at the end of the day, you know well that all the pressure of the world is on you. It's your wedding, and you are calling the shots. If something does not turn out the way you wanted it to, you will lament that mishap for the rest of your life.

At a certain point in time, you need to think of your wedding as a big project that you need to undertake. As is the case with any other project, you need to be aware of all the resources and ways in which you can turn this event into a hugely successful one.

Wedding crafts is a term that you have probably heard of before. When your wedding's only a month away, you need to do a lot more than simply be acquainted with that term. The best weddings are often the ones that put on the best wedding crafts on display.

There are hundreds, and perhaps thousands of wedding crafts that you can be well versed in. Each one beautifies the wedding in a different way. Some of the wedding crafts are simple, while others are strenuous. Contrary to popular belief, wedding crafts are not simply confined to centrepieces and flowers. There is so much more to it.

Luckily for you, you don't have to go to dozens of wedding planners or skim through hundreds of wedding trends magazines. We have prepared 43 of the finest wedding crafts that you can put to use on your special day.

So, without further ado, let's dive straight into the world of creative wedding madness.

1. The Aristocratic Arbor

The best place to start with is the backdrop. There is a wide array of options when it comes to decorating the backdrop and creating the perfect background for your beautiful wedding stage. We begin with the arbor.

Materials

- Ribbons

- Wooden Arbor

- Flowers

- Paint or Wooden Stain

- Burlap

Directions

1. Fix the arbor in a large open space. Paint the arbor to match your wedding theme.

2. Use the ribbons and flowers to decorate the arbor. Ribbons should be tied around the posts and the flowers should be attached to the bar. This is done to give the arbor a traditional look.

3. For a classy rustic look, tie a little burlap on the arbour.

2. Fabric of Your Choice

Materials

- Fabric strips, preferably satin or lace

- 5 to 6 String Lights

- Around 20 pillar candles

Directions

1. To make the backdrop look elegant and traditional at the same time, decorate it with satin or lace strips. Make sure the strips are pulled all the way down.

2. To make the highlight the color of the fabric strips, use string lights.

3. For further lighting and eye-catching decoration, place a number of identical pillar candles at the bottom of the backdrop.

3. Fluffy Feather

Materials

- Jute Twine

- A few handfuls of feathers, preferably those that are shaded

- A couple of strips of white lace

- A bunch of small sized white flowers

- 4-5 crystal accents or elevated candles

Directions

1. Use the jute twine to tie the feathers together.

2. Decorate the altar with white satin and white flowers to pull off a "heavenly angelic" look.

3. For better lighting, place the crystal accents or the elevated candles close to the altar.

4. Green Is Not Your Enemy

Materials

- A huge amount of moist, green and fresh leaves

- White lace fabric

- Eucalyptus garlands

- Pollen grains

Directions

1. String the leaves together and twirl them around your altar.

2. Take a handful of leaves and sprinkle them generously on your aisle. Attach a few eucalyptus garlands on your altar.

3. Spread pollen grains generously just in front of the altar. To create a contrast, wrap the altar with white lace.

5. Old School Chalk Board

Materials

- A huge chalkboard, preferably rectangle in shape. A 4 x 8' plywood

- Masonite would be ideal

- Shabby Chic Chalk Style Paint

- Pastel Colors

Directions

1. Place the chalkboard at the altar, make sure it stands vertical without toppling over.

2. Use the Shabby Chic Chalk Style Paint to write the names of the wedded couple, the date of the wedding and a few lovely quotes.

3. Use the pastel colors to draw and color fabulous designs. It's better to keep the colours confined to black and white.

I have included a bonus just for you…

FOR A LIMITED TIME ONLY – Get my best-selling book "DIY Crafts: The 100 Most Popular Crafts & Projects That Make Your Life Easier" absolutely FREE!

Readers who have downloaded the bonus book as well have seen the greatest changes in their crafting abilities and have expanded their repertoire of crafts – so it is *highly recommended* to get this bonus book today!

Get your free copy at:

ArtsCraftsAndMore.com/Bonus

6. Flowers to The Rescue

Materials

- A bucket of colorful flowers, especially those that match wedding themes such as white, pink, red and yellow

- A huge green floral wall

- Ribbons of the same color as the flowers

Directions

1. Put up the floral wall and stud flowers on the wall meticulously. Each layer of flowers should have a different hue.

2. Attach the ribbons alongside the flowers of the same color. Create a favorite quote with the flowers or mould them into attractive patterns.

7. Light It Up

Materials

- More than 30 odd string lights (The light bulbs should exude a bright glow)

- 3 Bouquets of flowers (Roses of different hues are recommended)

- Garlands of white flowers

Directions

1. Set up the string lights. Pack them together, till they look like a glowing backdrop.

2. Place the bouquets of roses at the front, and on either side of the altar.

3. Attach the garlands of white flowers at the top of the string lights.

8. The Holy Knots

Materials

- Around 5 to 6 pieces of very long ropes. Make sure the ropes are not too thin or too thick

- Ribbons, preferably of the same color as the ropes

- Large patches of fresh green leaves combined with wilting brown ones

- Large flowers preferably of a pink shade. Pink roses would be ideal in this situation

Directions

1. Tie up the rose in a number of different knots. Make sure the knots are big and visible.

2. The Ribbons should be tied in knots as well. Place the greenery and the flowers on top of the ropes and the ribbons.

9. As Clear as Crystal

Materials

- Sparkling crystal curtains of the very best quality

- A low hanging tree branch located outdoors

- A selection of creamy white flowers

Directions

1. Hang the crystal curtains on the low hanging tree branch outside.

2. Attach the creamy white flowers at the center of the crystal curtains.

3. Sprinkle some of the flowers on the altar and the aisle.

10. Rosy Red Rosettes

Materials

- An abundant supply of thin, crisp and striking paper rosettes in colors of red, orange and pink

- Paper pom poms of the same color as the paper rosettes

- A wooden rectangular wall

Directions

1. Affix the paper rosettes on the wooden wall. Make the patterns random for the best look.

2. The paper pom pomps can be placed in between the paper rosettes. Make sure pom poms of the same color are not clustered together.

11. Petals of Perfection

Your aisle needs as much attention as the altar. Here are some spectacular ways to dress up your aisle.

Materials

- Fall leaves that are crispy enough to crunch under footsteps

- Sufficient supply of petals. Strive for as much diversity in color as possible (Red, pink, orange, white and yellow petals are highly recommended)

- Flower heads of the same color as the petals

- Fabric of golden, white or pink hues

- Feathers, preferably multi-coloured

Directions

1. Place the petals on the aisle in particular patterns or shapes. You can look to make a monogram or simply form a blanket of petals.

2. Place the fabric in patches all over the bed of petals.

3. Sprinkle the flower heads, feather and fall leaves over the petals.

12. In Black and White

Materials

- A very long piece of cloth. The color of the cloth should be either black or white

- Paintbrushes of different sizes and differently shaped ends

- Black or white paint

- Petals of black and white roses

Directions

1. Place the piece of cloth along the entire length of the aisle.

2. Use the paintbrush and the paint to write quotes that characterize your wedding. Sprinkle the petals lightly over the cloth.

13. Bordering Candles

Materials

- A good amount of pillar sized candles, that measure up just below the knee length

- Smaller candles to complement the pillar sized candles

- Floral arrangements

- Small cylinder vases

- Wood slices embellished with moss

Directions

1. Border the edges of the aisle with the pillar-sized candles.

2. Place the smaller candles in between the pillar-sized candles. Put them atop the wood slices.

3. Decorate the pillar-sized candle with flowers. Place the pillar sized candles on the small cylinder vases.

14. Luminescent Lanterns

Materials

- Lanterns of various shapes. Make sure that no more than 3 are identical

- Burlap and lace, preferably of a white color

- Stanchions of medium length

- Flowers of the same color as the burlap and lace

Directions

1. Hang the lanterns from the stanchions.

2. Dress the lanterns up with the burlap and the lace.

3. Sprinkle some of the flowers on top of the lanterns, and spread the remaining over the aisle.

15. Dress Up the Chairs

Materials

- Sashes for the chairs. Have some extra in case a few tear up. They should be pink in color

- Flowers (The color of the flowers should be somewhat contrasting to that of the sashes)

- Crystal accents. Once again, the color should be different from the sashes

- Lightweight mason jars

- Colorful bouquets

Directions

1. Tie the sashes on all the chairs surrounding the aisle.

2. Attach the flowers and the crystal accents on the sashes.

3. Attach the lightweight mason jars on the chairs and fill them up with the color bouquets.

16. Illuminated Blossoms

Now for a list of centrepiece ideas that will literally blow you away

Materials

- Tight, long and strong ribbons. The ribbons should be of an imposing color

- Hanging candleholders (These should be identical in color and shape)

- Votive holders for the table

- Flower petals of the same color as the ribbons

- Small pieces of flowers clumped together

Directions

1. Use the ribbon to suspend the flowers from the ceiling.

2. Place the hanging candleholders in between the suspended flowers.

3. Sprinkle the petals on the votive holders.

17. Play with the Lights

Materials

- A good amount of paper lanterns. The number should be enough to fill the room

- A similar number of hanging bulbs (Keep a few extra just in case)

- Silver candle holders of the best quality

- Galvanized buckets

- White flowers

Directions

1. Hang the paper lanterns from the ceiling. Place the hanging light bulbs in between the lanterns. Suspend the silver candleholders from the ceiling.

2. On the table, place the galvanized buckets and fill them up with flowers.

18. Sparkle Brighter

Materials

- Rods and bars that can be hung to form a canopy structure.

- String lights (similar to the ones used during Christmas)

- Leafy garlands

- White lace strips

Directions

1. Wrap the lace strips around the bars.

2. Attach the string lights to the lace strips. Make sure there is enough to stretch to every corner of the canopy. Suspend the leafy garlands and wrap them around with some of the string lights.

33

19. A Terracotta Wedding

Materials

- Terracotta pots (They should be decently sized and strong enough to be stuffed with flowers)

- Colorful bouquets (Go for flowers that have really bold colors)

- Gold mercury glass candle holders

- Long stretches of burlap for the table

- Floral accents in plenty

Directions

1. Suspend the terracotta pots from the ceiling and stuff them with the bouquets.

2. Place the remaining pots on the table and fill them up with floral accents.

3. Gold mercury glass candleholders should also be suspended from the ceiling.

20. Playful Balloons

Materials

- Balloons of various sizes that float in the air. Make sure the colors are not too bright (Light shades of yellow and white go really well)

- Strings or ropes

- Wine or champagne bucket

Directions

1. Tie the larger balloons on the tables. Make sure the strings are well attached.

2. Place the champagne buckets at the centre of each table. Tie the smaller balloons to the champagne buckets.

21. The Breezy Seats

The chairs cannot be neglected in a wedding. The guests deserve a beautiful seating arrangement. Here's a list of seven to help you out.

Materials

- Wide ribbon in pastel shades (The colors you should be looking for are green, light pink, light turquoise or creamy peach)

- Wooden chairs with white cushions

- Sand from the beach

Directions

1. Sprinkle the sand lightly over the chair cushions. Make sure that you don't pile them up.

2. Tie the ribbons at the back of the chair. Affix 6 ribbons on each chair.

Check out Kitty's books at:

ArtsCraftsAndMore.com/go/books

22. Good Old Country Style

Materials

- Wooden chairs that are painted white

- White strips of burlap that have good width

- Wide strips of lace ribbon that are of a similar color as the burlap

- Dried baby's breath

Directions

1. Tie the burlap and the ribbon into a knot at the back of the chair.

2. Place the dried baby's breath just behind the knots to further beautify the chairs.

23. The Blissful Touch of Tulle

Materials

- An abundant supply of smooth, velvety and scented tulle fabric. Ivory tulle will be most ideal

- Satin ribbon of a darker hue than the tulle

- Good amounts of millinery flowers

- Gold tinted metal chairs

Directions

1. Wrap the tulle all around the back of the chair.

2. Use the satin ribbon to tie the fabric into a cute little knot.

3. Attach the millinery flower for a deft touch.

24. Storytelling Chairs

Materials

- Small chalkboards (About the half the length of the chairs in use)

- Metal chairs of the same color as the chalkboard

- Satin ribbons of a creamy white hue

- Eucalyptus branches clumped together in bunches

- White chalk for writing

Directions

1. Attach the chalkboard at the back of each and every single chair.

2. Write a small quote on each chair. The quotes can be written in pairs using two chairs.

3. Wrap the satin ribbon at the top corner of the chairs. Attach the eucalyptus branches on the white satin ribbon.

25. Twisted Wreaths of Love

Materials

- Plenty of grapevine wreaths that are dry and greyish brown in color

- Wooden chairs (painted in beige and topped with white cushions)

- Pink roses moist with dew drops

Directions

1. The grapevine wreathes should be shaped into hearts and then tied to the chairs.

2. The pink roses can be attached to the wreaths once they have been tied to the back of the chairs.

26. Sparkling Chair Vase

Materials

- A glass vase made of a jar (It's better if the jars are tiny and cute)

- Small powdery flowers that are still attached to their stems

- Wide caspia branches

- White roses (the amount should be triple that of the amount of vases)

- White lace ribbons

- Old school white wooden chairs

Directions

1. Attach the jars to the chairs with the white lace ribbons.

2. Stuff the powdery flowers, the white roses and the caspia branches inside the vases.

27. The Leafy Chairs

Materials

- Magnolia leaf garlands

- Jasmine flowers

- White satin ribbons

- Golden metal chairs with white cushions

- White rose petals

Directions

1. The magnolia leaf garlands should be placed at the back of each chair.

2. Plant the jasmine flowers on the leafy garlands. Sprinkle the petals of the white roses on the cushions of the chair.

28. The Tower of Light

The cake is one of the most significant emblems of the wedding. Therefore, getting the cake stand right is absolutely crucial.

Materials

- A 3-tiered dessert stand of medium height

- At least 30 to 40 different clear cups

- Votive candles of a white hue

Directions

1. Set up the 3-tiered dessert stand on a table.

2. Stuff the votive candles inside the clear cups one by one. Carefully place the clear cups on the 3 tiers of the dessert stand.

29. The Love Nest

Materials

- A single layered cake stand that has a wide surface area (These are usually known as bunny cake stands)

- Strips of raffia

- Dozen decorative, colorful eggs

Directions

1. Place the bunny stand on the table. Lay the strips off raffia carefully on top of the stand.

2. Place the eggs on top of the raffia to pull off the perfect Easter -themed cake stand.

30. The Garden-Fresh Look

Materials

- A cupcake stand that is pretty large in length and width (This stand can be of any color but green is highly recommended)

- Plenty of artificial succulents (These are easily available in the market)

- Preserved moss (Enough to have a striking presence in each cake stand)

Directions

1. Fill up the cupcake stand with succulents of different sizes, shapes and hues.

2. Place the preserved moss in between the succulents. Make sure they stand out and are of a color that contrasts with that of the artificial succulents.

31. Neat and Tidy

Materials

- A single layered cake stand of a pasty green color

- A green handkerchief

- A bottled liquid hand wash (It's recommended you buy a green one)

- A green sponge

- A bar of green hued soap

Directions

1. Place the handkerchief on top of the cake stand.

2. Place the bar of soap on top of the handkerchief. The sponge should be placed vertically right behind the bar of soap.

3. The liquid hand wash should be a few inches away from the rest of the items, and voila! You have a squeaky-clean washroom themed cake stand.

32. Domed Goodies

Materials

- Dome cake stands of varying shapes and sizes (The colors can also vary but should be similar to each other. Such as, the pink domed cake stand with a purple one)

- Chalk paints

Directions

1. Place the dome cake stands haphazardly on the table. Keep the small ones at the front and the big ones at the back.

2. Use the chalk paints to color the dome cake stands as you please.

33. The Stand of Herbs

Materials

- A wooden dessert stand of three layers

- Small clay pots filled with soil and lush growing herbs

- A bundle of small leaves

Directions

1. Stack the clay pots on each layer of the wooden desert stand.

2. Sprinkle the leaves on the soil of the clay pots, on the layers of the cake wooden stand as well as around the entire decoration piece.

34. The Elegant Floral Ball

Materials

- A huge bouquet of flowers preferably of the lighter hues such as pink, white, light blue etc

- A single layered dessert stand tinted with gold and of metallic make

- Strings of crystal beads

Directions

1. Place the bouquet on top of the cake stand. Make sure that the flowers are shaped into an enormous ball. Such shapes can be found easily at the florist, but you could also mould one yourself using scissors and tapes.

2. Attach the string of crystals at the bottom of the bouquet.

35. The Holiday Frenzy

Materials

- A single layered white cake stand

- About a dozen medium sized decoration spheres (ones used beneath the Christmas tree)

- A mini sized artificial Christmas tree with silver confetti leaves

- Paint

Directions

1. Place the balls on the roof of the cake stand. Make sure they are painted and gleaming.

2. Carefully place the Christmas tree at the centre of the crowd of spheres.

36. A Pleasing Bath

Materials

- A ceramic stand with scalloped edge (Make sure that the stand is white)

- Mason jars of varying sizes (The lids can be multi coloured if you are into bright colors)

- Cotton balls

- Travel-size toothpastes

Directions

1. Place the mason jars carefully on the ceramic stand. Make sure you don't overcrowd the stand.

2. Fill the mason jars up with cotton balls first, and then travel-size toothpastes.

37. The Citrus Flair

Materials

- A simple, white desert stand with a very flat surface

- White ceramic plates with golden edges

- A galvanized bucket

- Preserved hydrangeas

- Lemons of varying colors and sizes

Directions

1. Place the lemons on top of the cake stand. 3 or 4 should be enough.

2. Stack the ceramic plates together and place them beside the cake stand. Fill the galvanized bucket with the preserved hydrangeas.

38. A Candy Fest

No wedding is complete without a fulfilling dessert bar. Here are some tips to create an awesome one.

Materials

- A small, white and wooden shelf

- Mason jars of varying sizes

- Paint and paintbrush

- Assortment of candies

Directions

1. Place the mason jars on the wooden shelf carefully.

2. Fill up the jars with the candies. Make sure the colors are evenly distributed. Paint the lid of the jars to match the color of the candies.

39. Pies on A Tray

Materials

- An assortment of pies in golden tinted trays

- A wooden cake stand big enough to hold at least two trays

- Golden tinted ribbons

Directions

1. Place the cake stands on a draped table.

2. Put the trays of pies on the cake stands.

3. Decorate the table with the gold tinted ribbons.

40. Wafflelicious Dessert Corner

Materials

- A waffle maker

- Galvanized buckets of different sizes

- Raspberries

- Strawberries

- Mason Jars

- Whipped cream and syrup

Directions

1. Place the waffle maker on a draped and have it surrounded with the galvanized buckets and mason jars.

2. Fill up the galvanized buckets with the strawberries and the raspberries.

3. Fill up the mason jars with syrup and syrup.

41. Ice Cream Paradise

Materials

- Huge glass goblets (Three or four will suffice)

- A variety of ice cream

- Mason jars

- Popular ice cream toppings

Directions

1. Place the glass goblets on a wooden table and fill them up with delicious ice cream.

2. Stuff the ice cream toppings on the mason jars and place the mason jars just in front of the glass goblets.

42. Pop Corn Treats

Materials

- Large bowls (Make them of different colors)

- Old school wooden cart

- Popcorn of different colors

- Small pieces of paper and crayons

Directions

1. Pour the popcorn into the large bowls. Place the popcorn bowls on the wooden cart.

2. Use the crayons and the pieces of paper to form nametags for the popcorn.

43. A Chocolaty Affair

Materials

- Large and small bowls (Make sure they are tinted with elegant dark hues)

- An assortment of chocolate

- Marshmallows

- Trays

Directions

1. Place the chocolate on the trays.

2. Fill up the bowls with molten chocolate and marshmallows.

Conclusion

In the hustle and bustle of perfecting the decor of your wedding altar, aisle, chairs, cake stands and dessert bar, you ought not to forget to enjoy your wedding.

Sure, wedding days are stressful and strenuous for most parts, but that does not mean you can have a little fun on your wedding. Even if some of the things do not go as planned, there is absolutely no reason to worry.

Chances are, if you stick to these aforementioned crafts, your wedding will turn out to be just fine, and you can rock the dance floor without apprehensions flooding your mind.

Last Chance to Get YOUR Bonus!

FOR A LIMITED TIME ONLY – Get my best-selling book "DIY Crafts: The 100 Most Popular Crafts & Projects That Make Your Life Easier " absolutely FREE!

Readers who have downloaded the bonus book as well have seen the greatest changes in their crafting abilities and have expanded their repertoire of crafts – so it is *highly recommended* to get this bonus book today!

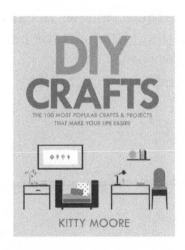

Get your free copy at:

ArtsCraftsAndMore.com/Bonus

Final Words

Thank you for downloading this book!

I really hope that you have been inspired to create your own projects and that you will have a lot of fun crafting.

I do hope that you and your family have found lots of ways to fill lazy afternoons or rainy days in a more fun way.

If you have enjoyed this book and would like to share your positive thoughts, could you please take 30 seconds of your time to go back and give me a review on my Amazon book page!

I really appreciate these reviews because I like to know what people have thought about the book.

Again, thank you and have fun crafting!

Disclaimer

No Warranties: The authors and publishers don't guarantee or warrant the quality, accuracy, completeness, timeliness, appropriateness or suitability of the information in this book, or of any product or services referenced by this site.

The information in this site is provided on an "as is" basis and the authors and publishers make no representations or warranties of any kind with respect to this information. This site may contain inaccuracies, typographical errors, or other errors.

Liability Disclaimer: The publishers, authors, and other parties involved in the creation, production, provision of information, or delivery of this site specifically disclaim any responsibility, and shall not be held liable for any damages, claims, injuries, losses, liabilities, costs, or obligations including any direct, indirect, special, incidental, or consequences damages (collectively known as "Damages") whatsoever and howsoever caused, arising out of, or in connection with the use or misuse of the site and the information contained within it, whether such Damages arise in contract, tort, negligence, equity, statute law, or by way of other legal theory.